GENERATIVE AI

A STEP-BY-STEP INTRODUCTION

RAHUL PANDIT

Contents

Preface

In recent years, Artificial Intelligence (AI) has transitioned from a theoretical pursuit to an integral part of our daily lives, revolutionizing industries and reshaping the way we interact with technology. At the forefront of this evolution is Generative AI, a subset of AI that not only analyzes data but also creates it—generating text, images, music, and even complex designs from scratch. What was once confined to science fiction has now become a reality, pushing the boundaries of creativity, innovation, and automation.

This book, "Demystifying Generative AI: A Step-by-Step Introduction," is designed to make this exciting technology accessible to a broad audience. Whether you are a curious reader, a professional exploring new AI-driven tools, or someone interested in understanding how machines can mimic human creativity, this book provides a comprehensive guide to the principles, models, and applications of generative AI.

Why This Book?

Generative AI is rapidly changing the landscape of multiple industries—from art and entertainment to healthcare and business. It has brought forth tools capable of writing novels, composing symphonies, and even aiding in drug discovery. However, as the power and potential of this technology expand, so do the challenges of understanding it. Through this book, I aim to break down complex concepts, making them approachable without sacrificing depth or detail.

This book will walk you through the foundational models that power generative AI, from GPT and GANs to newer approaches like diffusion models. You'll see how these models are applied in real-world contexts, from virtual assistants to AI-generated art. We'll also cover essential topics like prompt engineering, the ethical dilemmas surrounding AI, and what the future might hold for this groundbreaking technology.

Who Is This Book For?

This book is written for a diverse audience:

- Non-technical readers seeking to grasp the core concepts and transformative impact of generative AI without needing to dive deep into coding or complex algorithms.
- Professionals in industries like marketing, healthcare, and content creation who are looking to harness the power of AI-driven tools in their work.
- Students and AI enthusiasts interested in learning about the models and principles behind cutting-edge technologies like GPT, DALL·E, and more.

Looking Ahead

As we embark on this journey into the realm of generative AI, we stand on the cusp of a new era—an era where machines can co-create with humans, blurring the lines between natural and artificial creativity. The possibilities are endless, and the impact of generative AI will continue to unfold in ways we cannot yet fully predict. My hope is that this book serves as a valuable guide to help you navigate this exciting frontier.

Let us dive into the world of generative AI, where imagination meets machine intelligence.

CHAPTER I

What is Generative AI?

Generative AI represents a significant frontier in the field of artificial intelligence, showcasing the remarkable ability of machines to understand, learn, and create new content. From text and images to music and code, generative AI systems can produce work that is not only functional but often indistinguishable from that created by humans. This introductory chapter provides an overview of generative AI, setting the foundation for deeper exploration into its mechanisms, applications, and ethical considerations.

1.1 Introduction to AI and Machine Learning

This section introduces the reader to the broader landscape of AI and machine learning before zooming in on generative AI.

- **A Brief History of AI:**

  - **1950s-1970s:** The early days of AI began with pioneers like Alan Turing, who proposed the Turing Test to measure machine intelligence. Early AI research focused on logic and problem-solving, with systems like ELIZA (a simple chatbot) emerging as basic conversational agents.
  - **1980s-2000s:** AI research shifted to knowledge-based systems and early forms of machine learning, where algorithms could learn from data. This era also saw the rise of symbolic AI, expert systems, and neural networks.

- ○ **2010s-2020s:** With advances in computing power, neural networks became more sophisticated, leading to deep learning breakthroughs. Companies like Google, OpenAI, and DeepMind began making significant strides in AI, setting the stage for modern generative AI models.

- **Machine Learning: The Engine of Modern AI:**

  - ○ **Supervised Learning:** Teaching AI models using labeled data to make predictions (e.g., classifying images of cats and dogs).
  - ○ **Unsupervised Learning:** Allowing AI to find hidden patterns in data without explicit labels (e.g., clustering customers based on their purchasing behavior).
  - ○ **Reinforcement Learning:** Training AI to make decisions in dynamic environments by rewarding it for desired actions (e.g., AlphaGo learning to master the game of Go).

- **How Deep Learning Unlocked New Possibilities:**

  - ○ Deep learning uses multi-layered neural networks that mimic the way the human brain processes information. This enabled AI to excel in tasks like image recognition, natural language processing, and, most importantly, content generation.

1.2 What is Generative AI?

This section provides a refined definition of Generative AI and examples of how it diverges from traditional AI models.

- **Generative AI vs. Discriminative AI:**

  - **Discriminative Models** focus on distinguishing between different classes of data (e.g., is this email spam or not?).
  - **Generative Models** learn to generate new instances of data, such as writing new text, composing music, or creating images.

- **Generative AI's Core Functionality:**

  - It works by understanding the underlying patterns of data (like text or images) and then creating new, similar content.
  - It doesn't memorize data but instead generalizes from patterns, allowing it to generate unique and coherent outputs.

- **Why is Generative AI Revolutionary?**

  - It democratizes creativity, allowing non-experts to generate content that would otherwise require specialized skills.
  - It augments human creativity by acting as a co-creator in fields like design, writing, and coding.
  - **Personalization at Scale:** It can generate highly personalized content, from tailored marketing messages to customized products.

1.3 Types of Generative AI Models

Here, the expanded focus will further explain the mechanics of each type of generative model, giving readers a clearer understanding of how they work under the hood.

- **Language Models (e.g., GPT, BERT, T5):**

  - **GPT (Generative Pre-trained Transformer):** These models use a transformer architecture to predict the next word in a sequence. GPT-3, for example, is trained on billions of text examples and can generate essays, code, dialogues, and more.

    - **How GPT Works:** It uses a process called autoregression, where it generates one word at a time, considering the context of previously generated words.
    - **BERT (Bidirectional Encoder Representations from Transformers):** Unlike GPT, which generates content, BERT is a bidirectional model that excels in understanding and extracting meaning from text, useful for comprehension tasks like question-answering.

  - **T5 (Text-to-Text Transfer Transformer):** T5 frames all NLP tasks as text-to-text problems, allowing it to generate output for tasks like summarization, translation, and question-answering.

- **Generative Adversarial Networks (GANs):**

  - **How GANs Work in Detail:**

    - **Generator:** This network produces new data (e.g., images) by learning from the training data.
    - **Discriminator:** This network evaluates the authenticity of the generated data, trying to distinguish it from real data.

- **Adversarial Process:** Over time, the generator improves as it tries to "fool" the discriminator, resulting in highly realistic outputs.

  - **Common GAN Applications:**

    - **Deepfake Creation:** GANs can synthesize realistic human faces or videos.
    - **Image Style Transfer:** GANs can apply the style of one image (e.g., a famous painting) to another (e.g., a photograph).
    - **Super-Resolution:** GANs can enhance the resolution of images by generating high-quality pixel details.

- **Variational Autoencoders (VAEs):**

  - **How VAEs Work:**

    - The encoder compresses input data (e.g., an image) into a lower-dimensional representation (a latent space), while the decoder reconstructs this compressed information back into a complete image.
    - **Key Advantage:** VAEs are great for generating smooth variations of data, making them useful in applications like face generation or data augmentation.

- **Diffusion Models:**

  - **How Diffusion Models Work:**

- These models generate data by gradually reversing a noise process. They are highly effective in image generation and have been shown to outperform GANs in certain tasks.
- **Applications:** Often used in cutting-edge AI art creation and improving image generation fidelity.

1.4 Expanded Real-World Examples of Generative AI

Add more examples of where generative AI is used today, showcasing its diverse applications across industries.

- **Content Creation:**

  - **Marketing and Social Media:** Generative AI tools like Jasper AI and Writesonic help marketers create blog posts, ad copy, and social media content at scale.
  - **Journalism:** Tools like OpenAI's GPT are being explored for news generation, summarizing articles, and even writing financial reports.
  - **Education:** AI-generated quizzes, personalized learning paths, and automated grading systems are becoming more common.

- **Art and Design:**

  - **AI-Generated Art:** Tools like DALL·E and MidJourney allow artists and designers to generate unique pieces of digital artwork based on text prompts.
  - **Fashion Design:** AI is now being used to create clothing designs, blending various styles and trends to come up with novel designs.

- **Video Game Development:**

  - **Procedural Generation:** Generative AI creates game levels, characters, and even entire game worlds, reducing the time developers need to create content manually.
  - **NPC Dialogue:** AI tools are being used to generate realistic dialogue for non-playable characters (NPCs) in games, adding depth to player interactions.

- **Healthcare and Medicine:**

  - **Drug Discovery:** Generative AI is assisting pharmaceutical companies in generating novel drug compounds by simulating molecular structures.
  - **Medical Imaging:** GANs and VAEs are improving the accuracy of medical scans by enhancing image quality and resolution.

- **Music and Audio Production:**

  - **AI-Generated Music:** Platforms like OpenAI's MuseNet and AIVA allow musicians and non-musicians alike to compose original music.
  - **Sound Design:** AI tools are used to generate sound effects for films and games, creating novel sounds that wouldn't be possible with traditional methods.

1.5 Expanded Types of Content Generated by AI
Go into more detail about the variety of content generative AI can create, focusing on key sectors.

- **Textual Content:**

- ◦ **Creative Writing:** AI can help authors draft storylines, character dialogues, and plot ideas, aiding in the creative writing process.
- ◦ **Technical Writing:** AI is increasingly used to generate code documentation, user manuals, and scientific research summaries.
- ◦ **Legal Document Drafting:** Some AI systems are designed to generate legal contracts, briefs, and reports.

- **Visual Content:**

  - ◦ **AI-Generated Logos and Branding:** Tools like Canva and Looka use generative algorithms to create professional logos and branding materials.
  - ◦ **Interior Design and Architecture:** Generative design tools are helping architects and interior designers visualize and create new spaces, optimizing them based on specific criteria (e.g., light, space usage).

- **Video and Animation:**

  - ◦ **AI-Generated Animations:** AI tools are being used to generate animated content, reducing manual labor in the animation industry.
  - ◦ **Deepfakes and CGI:** AI models can generate highly realistic synthetic videos, though this technology raises significant ethical concerns (to be addressed in later chapters).

1.6 The Future of Generative AI

Expand on the broader impact generative AI will have across multiple industries.

- **Creative Professions Augmented by AI:**

  - The creative process, traditionally the realm of human intuition, will increasingly be supported by AI co-creators, helping artists, writers, and designers work faster and more effectively.

- **Hyper-Personalization:**

  - In industries like marketing and entertainment, generative AI will enable companies to tailor experiences down to the individual level, from personalized movies to hyper-targeted advertising.

- **The Evolution of Human-AI Collaboration:**

  - We're moving toward an era where humans and AI work side by side. AI will handle mundane tasks, allowing humans to focus on higher-level creativity and decision-making.

- **Challenges Ahead:**

  - **Ethics and Misuse:** As AI-generated content becomes indistinguishable from human-created content, there are ethical concerns around deepfakes, misinformation, and intellectual property theft.
  - **Regulation and Governance:** Future chapters will explore how governments and organizations will

need to create policies that manage the risks associated with generative AI.

Summary of this Chapter:

- Expanded understanding of AI's evolution, and the significance of generative AI in various fields.
- Introduced deeper mechanics of different generative models like GPT, GANs, and diffusion models.
- Provided more real-world examples and types of content generated by AI across industries.
- Discussed the future potential and challenges generative AI poses in creativity, personalization, and ethics.

CHAPTER II

The Foundations of Generative Models

Generative models have revolutionized the field of artificial intelligence by enabling machines to not only recognize patterns but to create entirely new content across various domains, from language to images. This chapter delves into the foundational concepts and technologies behind these models, examining their types, architectures, and applications. We begin with an overview of generative models and how they differ from discriminative models, exploring key concepts such as probability distributions and latent variables. From there, we take a deeper look at the most important generative models today—language models like GPT, BERT, and T5, adversarial networks such as GANs, variational autoencoders (VAEs), and the emerging diffusion models. Finally, we explore how generative models work, emphasizing the importance of large datasets, contextual understanding, and embeddings in producing coherent and contextually relevant outputs. By understanding these building blocks, we gain insight into the powerful capabilities of generative AI and its growing impact across multiple industries.

2.1 Overview of Generative Models

- **Types of Generative Models:**

  - **Generative Models vs. Discriminative Models:**

    - **Generative Models:** These models generate new data instances that resemble a given dataset. They learn the joint probability distribution $P(x,y)P(x,y)P(x,y)$ and can generate new samples by sampling from this distribution.

- **Discriminative Models:** These models focus on modeling the conditional probability $P(y \mid x)P(y \mid x)P(y \mid x)$ and are used for classification or regression tasks. They predict outcomes based on input data rather than generating new data.

- **Key Concepts:**

  - **Probability Distributions:** Generative models learn to estimate the probability distribution of the data. They use this learned distribution to generate new instances that are statistically similar to the training data.
  - **Latent Variables:** Many generative models introduce latent variables that capture underlying factors of variation in the data. These variables help the model generate diverse and realistic samples.

- **Generative vs. Discriminative Examples:**

  - **Text Generation (Generative):** GPT models generate new text based on learned language patterns.
  - **Image Classification (Discriminative):** Models like ResNet classify images into categories without generating new images.

- **Benefits of Generative Models:**

- ○ **Creativity and Innovation:** They enable new forms of creative expression by generating art, music, and other media.
- ○ **Data Augmentation:** They can create synthetic data to supplement real datasets, improving the performance of other models.
- ○ **Personalization:** They generate personalized content tailored to individual preferences and needs.

2.2 Language Models (GPT, BERT, T5)

- **Detailed Architectures:**

  - ○ **GPT (Generative Pre-trained Transformer):**

    - ▪ **Self-Attention Mechanism:** The self-attention mechanism in GPT allows the model to weigh the importance of different words in a sequence when generating text. This attention mechanism helps GPT understand context and produce coherent responses.
    - ▪ **Transformer Blocks:** GPT uses multiple transformer blocks, each consisting of self-attention layers and feedforward neural networks. These blocks capture different levels of linguistic patterns.
    - ▪ **Pre-training Objectives:** GPT is trained with unsupervised learning objectives, such as predicting the next word in a sentence. This allows the model to learn general language representations before fine-tuning on specific tasks.

- ○ **BERT (Bidirectional Encoder Representations from Transformers):**

  - ▪ **Bidirectional Contextualization:** BERT's bidirectional approach allows it to consider both preceding and following words in a sentence, leading to a deeper understanding of context compared to unidirectional models.
  - ▪ **Training Tasks:**

    - ▪ **Masked Language Modeling (MLM):** Randomly masks words in a sentence and trains the model to predict them based on context.
    - ▪ **Next Sentence Prediction (NSP):** Trains the model to predict whether one sentence follows another in a given text, enhancing its ability to understand sentence relationships.

- ○ **T5 (Text-to-Text Transfer Transformer):**

  - ▪ **Unified Framework:** T5 treats all NLP tasks as text-to-text problems, which means input and output are both text. This unified approach simplifies task formulation and allows the model to transfer knowledge across tasks.
  - ▪ **Pre-training Tasks:** T5 is pre-trained on a diverse set of tasks, such as translation and summarization, which helps it generalize well to various applications.

- **Fine-Tuning and Transfer Learning:**

- **Fine-Tuning:** After pre-training on large datasets, these models are fine-tuned on specific tasks using labeled data. Fine-tuning adapts the pre-trained model to the nuances of the target task.
- **Transfer Learning:** The ability to leverage pre-trained models for new tasks is known as transfer learning. It allows practitioners to use existing models as a starting point, reducing the amount of task-specific data needed.

- **Real-World Applications:**

  - **Customer Service:** Language models are used in chatbots and virtual assistants to handle customer queries and provide support.
  - **Content Creation:** Automating the creation of articles, blog posts, and social media content.
  - **Education:** Providing tutoring and personalized learning experiences through interactive dialogue systems.

2.3 GANs (Generative Adversarial Networks)

- **Detailed Components:**

  - **Generator Network:**

    - **Architecture:** The generator network creates synthetic data by transforming random noise into data samples. It learns to produce realistic data by comparing its outputs to real data.
    - **Loss Function:** The generator's loss function is designed to maximize the probability that the

discriminator will classify its generated data as real.

- ○ **Discriminator Network:**

  - **Architecture:** The discriminator network evaluates data samples and determines whether they are real or generated. It learns to distinguish between genuine and fake data.
  - **Loss Function:** The discriminator's loss function aims to minimize classification errors, effectively distinguishing real data from fake data.

- **Adversarial Training Dynamics:**

  - ○ **Training Process:** During training, the generator and discriminator engage in a game where the generator improves its ability to generate realistic data while the discriminator enhances its ability to detect fakes.
  - ○ **Convergence:** The goal is for both networks to reach a point where the generator produces data that is indistinguishable from real data, and the discriminator cannot reliably distinguish between real and generated data.

- **Challenges in GAN Training:**

  - ○ **Mode Collapse:** The generator may produce a limited variety of samples, reducing diversity in generated data.
  - ○ **Training Instability:** GANs can suffer from instability issues, such as oscillations in training loss, requiring careful tuning of hyperparameters and

training procedures.

- **Applications of GANs:**

  - **Art and Design:** Generating artwork, designing fashion, and creating virtual environments.
  - **Medical Imaging:** Enhancing medical images and generating synthetic medical data for research and diagnostics.
  - **Entertainment:** Creating realistic characters and scenes in video games and movies.

2.4 VAEs (Variational Autoencoders)

- **Detailed Components:**

  - **Encoder Network:**

    - **Architecture:** The encoder maps input data to a latent space representation. It outputs parameters for a probability distribution, such as mean and variance, that define the latent variables.
    - **Latent Space Representation:** The encoder compresses input data into a lower-dimensional latent space, capturing essential features and variations.

  - **Decoder Network:**

    - **Architecture:** The decoder reconstructs data from the latent space representation. It learns to generate new data that resembles the original input.

- **Reconstruction Loss:** Measures the quality of the data reconstruction, ensuring that the decoder accurately reproduces the original data.

- **Training VAEs:**

  - **Objective Function:** The training objective is to minimize a combination of reconstruction loss and KL divergence.

    - **Reconstruction Loss:** Ensures that the generated data is close to the original data.
    - **KL Divergence:** Regularizes the latent space to follow a specific distribution, ensuring smooth and coherent data generation.

- **Applications of VAEs:**

  - **Image Generation:** Creating new images by sampling from the latent space.
  - **Feature Learning:** Learning meaningful features from data that can be used for downstream tasks.
  - **Anomaly Detection:** Identifying outliers by comparing the reconstruction error of data instances.

2.5 Diffusion Models

- **Detailed Mechanisms:**

  - **Forward Diffusion Process:**

- **Noise Addition:** The forward process involves progressively adding noise to data over several steps, transforming it into a noise distribution.
- **Noise Schedule:** Controls the rate and amount of noise added at each step, influencing the quality and variability of generated data.

- **Reverse Diffusion Process:**

  - **Denoising:** The reverse process learns to remove noise from corrupted data, reconstructing the original data distribution.
  - **Training Objective:** The model is trained to predict the noise at each step, minimizing the difference between predicted and actual noise.

- **Training Diffusion Models:**

  - **Objective Function:** The training objective involves minimizing a loss function that measures the difference between predicted and actual noise, guiding the model to accurately reverse the diffusion process.
  - **Training Techniques:** Techniques like stochastic gradient descent are used to optimize the model's parameters.

- **Applications of Diffusion Models:**

  - **High-Resolution Image Generation:** Producing detailed and realistic images from noisy inputs.
  - **Text-to-Image Generation:** Creating images based on textual descriptions, combining language and

visual synthesis.

2.6 How Generative Models Work

- **Training Large Datasets:**

  - **Data Requirements:** Generative models often require extensive datasets to learn complex patterns and generate high-quality content. Large datasets provide diverse examples, helping models generalize well.
  - **Scalability:** Training large models on large datasets requires significant computational resources, including GPUs or TPUs, and efficient data management strategies.

- **The Importance of Context and Embeddings:**

  - **Contextual Understanding:** For generative models to produce relevant and coherent outputs, they need to understand the context of input data. This involves considering the surrounding context to generate appropriate responses or outputs.
  - **Embeddings:**

    - **Text Embeddings:** In NLP, word embeddings capture semantic meanings and relationships between words. Techniques like Word2Vec, GloVe, and BERT embeddings represent words as dense vectors in a continuous space.
    - **Image Embeddings:** In computer vision, image embeddings capture visual features and characteristics. These embeddings enable models

to generate or manipulate images based on learned representations.

- **Applications of Context and Embeddings:**

  ◦ **Language Models:** Use embeddings to understand and generate text that is contextually relevant.
  ◦ **Image Generation:** Leverage embeddings to create images that align with specific attributes or descriptions.
  ◦ **Cross-Modal Applications:** Combine text and image embeddings to generate content that integrates information from multiple modalities.

Summary of this Chapter:

- **Overview of Generative Models:** Detailed the types of generative models and their differences from discriminative models, including their applications and benefits.
- **Language Models (GPT, BERT, T5):** Explored the architecture, training, and applications of major language models.
- **GANs (Generative Adversarial Networks):** Covered the components, training dynamics, and applications of GANs.
- **VAEs (Variational Autoencoders):** Detailed the architecture, training, and use cases of VAEs.
- **Diffusion Models:** Introduced the mechanisms, training, and applications of diffusion models.
- **How Generative Models Work:** Explained the training of large datasets and the role of context and embeddings in generative models.

CHAPTER III

Applications of Generative AI Across Industries

Generative AI is driving profound changes across a wide range of industries, reshaping how businesses operate, content is created, and even how healthcare is delivered. From text creation to image generation, music composition, business automation, and healthcare innovation, AI is opening new possibilities for efficiency, creativity, and problem-solving. This chapter explores the diverse applications of generative AI, highlighting its transformative impact in each field. We begin with its role in text generation, where AI-powered chatbots and content creators are automating customer service, producing personalized content, and crafting creative narratives. We then move into the visual arts, discussing how AI is revolutionizing art and design by enabling the generation of stunning visuals, product designs, and media content. Additionally, we explore AI's impact on music and audio generation, where it collaborates with human composers and creates adaptive, interactive soundscapes. The chapter also covers how AI is enhancing business operations by streamlining workflows, automating marketing tasks, and improving data analysis. Finally, we look at the groundbreaking advancements generative AI is making in healthcare, where it assists in drug discovery, medical imaging, and diagnostics. Through this examination, we uncover how generative AI is becoming a driving force behind innovation in nearly every sector.

3.1 Generative AI in Text Creation

Generative AI's capabilities in text creation are not just transforming how content is produced but also how human-computer interactions are evolving.

- **Chatbots and Virtual Assistants:**

  - **Natural Language Understanding (NLU):** NLU allows chatbots and virtual assistants to comprehend user input in a nuanced way. By using models like GPT-4, these systems can parse intent, recognize entities, and generate relevant responses.

    - **Intent Recognition:** AI systems can identify the purpose behind a user's query, whether it's seeking information, requesting assistance, or performing a specific task.
    - **Entity Recognition:** Extracting specific information from user input, such as names, dates, or locations, to provide precise answers or execute commands.

  - **Applications:**

    - **Customer Service:** AI-driven chatbots can handle routine customer inquiries, process service requests, and provide troubleshooting guidance. They reduce wait times and operational costs while improving customer experience.
    - **Healthcare Assistance:** Virtual assistants can help with scheduling appointments, providing medical information, and offering support for managing health conditions.

- **Travel and Hospitality:** AI can assist with booking reservations, providing travel recommendations, and offering real-time updates on travel conditions.

- **Content Generation:**

  - **Automated Article Writing:** AI can produce news articles, blog posts, and technical papers by analyzing large volumes of data and generating text that adheres to specific editorial guidelines.

    - **Data-Driven Reporting:** Generating reports and summaries from structured data, such as financial statements or research findings, with human-like readability.
    - **Content Personalization:** Tailoring articles and posts to align with individual reader preferences based on their behavior and interests.

  - **Creative Writing:**

    - **Plot and Character Development:** AI tools can assist authors by suggesting plot ideas, character traits, and dialogue, enhancing creativity and overcoming writer's block.
    - **Interactive Storytelling:** Creating interactive narratives for games and educational tools, where the story evolves based on user choices and interactions.

  - **Social Media:**

- **Engagement Optimization:** Generative AI can craft engaging social media posts, hashtags, and multimedia content that resonate with specific audiences, boosting engagement and brand visibility.
- **Real-Time Content Creation:** Generating timely and relevant content in response to current events, trends, or user-generated content.

3.2 Image and Art Creation

Generative AI's role in image and art creation is revolutionizing visual content, offering new creative tools and possibilities.

- **AI Art:**

  - **Style Transfer:**

    - **Algorithmic Approaches:** Techniques like neural style transfer use convolutional neural networks (CNNs) to apply artistic styles to images. This involves separating and recombining content and style representations.
    - **Real-Time Style Transfer:** Implementing real-time style transfer in applications like live video streaming, where users can apply artistic effects to their video feeds.

  - **Creative Generation:**

    - **Generative Adversarial Networks (GANs):** GANs can generate photorealistic images and artworks by learning from large datasets of existing art. They can create new compositions or mimic the style of famous artists.

- **Artistic Exploration:** AI tools enable artists to experiment with novel styles and forms, combining traditional techniques with machine-generated aesthetics.

- **Design:**

  - **Product Design:**

    - **Generative Design:** AI algorithms optimize design solutions by exploring numerous design variations based on specified constraints and goals, such as weight, strength, and material efficiency.
    - **Customization:** AI can create custom designs for products, such as personalized consumer goods, based on individual preferences and usage data.

  - **Graphic Design:**

    - **Automated Layouts:** AI tools can generate layouts for websites, brochures, and advertisements, automating tasks like font selection, color schemes, and spacing.
    - **Creative Assistance:** AI can suggest design elements and arrangements, enhancing the creative process and allowing designers to focus on high-level concepts.

- **Visual Content Production:**

- **Media and Entertainment:**

  - **CGI and Special Effects:** AI is used to create realistic visual effects and CGI characters in films and video games, enhancing storytelling with high-quality visuals.
  - **Virtual Reality (VR) and Augmented Reality (AR):** Generative AI contributes to creating immersive environments and interactive experiences in VR and AR applications.

- **Personalized Content:**

  - **Avatar Creation:** AI can generate personalized avatars and profile pictures based on user input and preferences, enhancing user engagement in digital spaces.
  - **Marketing Materials:** Designing personalized marketing materials, such as banners and advertisements, tailored to individual customer profiles and behaviors.

3.3 Music and Audio Generation

Generative AI is reshaping the music and audio industries by introducing innovative ways to create and manipulate sound.

- **AI-Generated Music:**

  - **Composition:**

    - **Algorithmic Composition:** AI models can compose original pieces by learning from various musical genres, structures, and patterns. They can generate melodies, harmonies, and rhythms that adhere to specific styles.

- **Collaborative Composition:** AI tools can collaborate with human composers, providing suggestions and generating musical ideas that complement human creativity.

- **Adaptive Music:**

  - **Interactive Soundtracks:** AI can create adaptive music that changes in response to user actions or environmental conditions in games and interactive media, enhancing the immersive experience.
  - **Personalized Playlists:** AI can generate personalized playlists and music recommendations based on user preferences and listening history.

- **Voice Synthesis:**

  - **Text-to-Speech (TTS):**

    - **Naturalness and Expressiveness:** Advances in TTS technology allow AI to generate speech with natural intonation, emotional expressiveness, and varied accents. This improves the realism and usability of virtual assistants and audiobooks.
    - **Multilingual Capabilities:** AI-driven TTS systems support multiple languages and dialects, making content accessible to a global audience.

- ○ **Voice Cloning:**

  - ▪ **Custom Voice Creation:** AI can replicate specific voices for use in media, entertainment, and personalized applications. This technology can create voiceovers for characters, narrators, or virtual personas.
  - ▪ **Ethical Considerations:** Voice cloning raises ethical concerns regarding consent, misuse, and deepfakes, necessitating guidelines and safeguards.

- **Sound Design:**

  - ○ **Generative Sound Effects:**

    - ▪ **New Sound Creation:** AI models can generate novel sound effects by learning from existing audio data and creating new auditory experiences for media and entertainment.
    - ▪ **Audio Enhancement:** AI can improve the quality of audio recordings by reducing background noise, enhancing clarity, and adjusting sound characteristics.

  - ○ **Audio Restoration:**

    - ▪ **Old Recordings:** Restoring and enhancing historical audio recordings, such as vintage music or archived speeches, by removing distortions and improving fidelity.

3.4 Business and Productivity Tools

Generative AI enhances business operations by streamlining workflows, optimizing marketing efforts, and improving data analysis.

- **Workflow Automation:**

  - **Process Automation:**

    - **Routine Tasks:** Automating repetitive tasks like data entry, email responses, and document management, freeing up human resources for more complex activities.
    - **Complex Workflows:** Integrating AI with RPA to handle complex workflows that involve multiple decision points and process variations.

  - **Intelligent Automation:**

    - **Decision-Making Support:** AI tools can assist in decision-making by analyzing data, generating insights, and recommending actions based on predefined criteria and objectives.
    - **Adaptive Workflows:** AI can adapt workflows in real-time based on changing conditions, optimizing processes and improving efficiency.

- **Marketing:**

  - **Content Creation:**

    - **Automated Copywriting:** Generating marketing copy, advertisements, and product descriptions based on brand guidelines and target audience characteristics.

- **Campaign Optimization:** Using AI to analyze campaign performance, identify trends, and optimize content for better engagement and conversion rates.

- **Customer Insights:**

  - **Behavior Analysis:** Analyzing customer data to generate insights into purchasing behavior, preferences, and trends. This information helps in crafting targeted marketing strategies.
  - **Predictive Modeling:** Forecasting customer needs and market trends using AI-driven predictive models, enabling proactive marketing and sales strategies.

- **Data Analysis:**

  - **Predictive Analytics:**

    - **Trend Forecasting:** Using AI to analyze historical data and predict future trends, such as sales forecasts, market demand, and customer behavior.
    - **Risk Assessment:** Identifying potential risks and opportunities based on predictive models, helping businesses make informed decisions.

  - **Natural Language Queries:**

    - **Data Exploration:** Allowing users to interact with data using natural language queries, making it easier to generate reports, explore datasets, and derive insights without requiring advanced technical skills.

3.5 Healthcare

Generative AI is making significant strides in healthcare by advancing drug discovery, enhancing medical imaging, and improving diagnostics.

- **Drug Discovery:**

  - **Molecular Design:**

    - **AI-Driven Discovery:** Generative models can design new drug candidates by analyzing chemical structures, predicting interactions, and optimizing molecular properties for efficacy and safety.
    - **Virtual Screening:** AI can perform virtual screening of large compound libraries, identifying promising drug candidates and accelerating the drug development process.

  - **Biological Simulations:**

    - **Molecular Dynamics:** Simulating molecular interactions and dynamics to predict drug behavior and optimize drug design.
    - **Disease Modeling:** Creating models of biological processes and disease mechanisms to understand drug effects and guide research.

- **Medical Imaging:**

- ○ **Image Enhancement:**

  - ▪ **Noise Reduction:** AI models can enhance the quality of medical images by reducing noise, improving resolution, and highlighting important features.
  - ▪ **Contrast Adjustment:** Enhancing image contrast to improve the visibility of anatomical structures and abnormalities.

- ○ **Image Analysis:**

  - ▪ **Automated Detection:** Using AI to detect and classify abnormalities in medical images, such as tumors, fractures, or lesions, improving diagnostic accuracy and speed.
  - ▪ **Predictive Diagnostics:** Analyzing imaging data to predict disease progression and patient outcomes, assisting in early intervention and personalized treatment.

- **Diagnostics:**

  - ○ **Predictive Modeling:**

    - ▪ **Patient Risk Assessment:** Using AI to predict patient risk for various conditions based on medical history, lifestyle factors, and genetic information.
    - ▪ **Outcome Prediction:** Forecasting treatment outcomes and disease progression to guide clinical decisions and treatment planning.

- ○ **Decision Support:**

    - **Clinical Decision Support Systems (CDSS):** AI-driven tools that provide recommendations and support to healthcare professionals based on patient data and clinical guidelines.
    - **Personalized Medicine:** Tailoring treatment plans to individual patients based on AI analysis of genetic, environmental, and lifestyle factors.

Summary of this Chapter:

- **Generative AI in Text Creation:** In-depth exploration of chatbots, content generation, and customer service automation.
- **Image and Art Creation:** Detailed discussion on AI art, design, and visual content production.
- **Music and Audio Generation:** Comprehensive look at AI-generated music, voice synthesis, and sound design.
- **Business and Productivity Tools:** Examination of AI's role in workflow automation, marketing, and data analysis.
- **Healthcare:** Thorough analysis of AI applications in drug discovery, medical imaging, and diagnostics.

CHAPTER IV

Key Generative AI Platforms and Tools

Generative AI is transforming the technological landscape, driven by platforms and tools that innovate and redefine the boundaries of creativity and functionality. From OpenAI's sophisticated language models to Google's expansive knowledge-based applications, these platforms are at the forefront of the AI revolution. This section delves into the world's leading generative AI tools, including OpenAI, Google's Bard, Microsoft Copilot, and others, highlighting their unique capabilities and the diverse applications they power. We will explore how these tools not only enhance productivity across various domains but also push the envelope on what artificial intelligence can achieve in areas such as art, science, and more. Through this exploration, we aim to provide a comprehensive understanding of the significant impact these platforms have on both the current and future states of AI technology.

4.1 OpenAI

OpenAI is a leader in the field of generative AI, developing models that have set benchmarks in natural language processing, image generation, and code assistance.

1. ChatGPT

- Overview:

    ◦ **ChatGPT** is a versatile conversational model based on the GPT architecture. It is designed to interact with users through natural language, understanding and generating human-like responses.

- **Technological Aspects:**

  - **Architecture:** ChatGPT utilizes the Transformer architecture, specifically the GPT-4 model. This architecture consists of multiple layers of attention mechanisms and feed-forward neural networks, allowing the model to process and generate text with high contextual awareness.
  - **Training Data:** Trained on a diverse range of internet text, ChatGPT learns to generate coherent and contextually relevant responses. It employs techniques such as unsupervised learning and reinforcement learning from human feedback (RLHF) to improve its conversational abilities.

- **Real-World Use Cases:**

  - **Customer Support:** Businesses integrate ChatGPT into customer service systems to handle FAQs, resolve issues, and provide 24/7 support. For example, e-commerce platforms use ChatGPT to assist customers with order inquiries and product recommendations.
  - **Education:** Educational platforms use ChatGPT to provide tutoring services, answer student queries, and support personalized learning. It can explain complex concepts, assist with homework, and offer study resources.
  - **Entertainment:** ChatGPT powers interactive storytelling and gaming experiences by generating dialogues and narrative elements. It can create

unique storylines based on user inputs, enhancing engagement in interactive fiction and role-playing games.

- **Features and Innovations:**

  - **Contextual Understanding:** ChatGPT maintains context across interactions, enabling it to provide relevant and coherent responses in extended conversations.
  - **Custom Instructions:** Users can provide specific instructions to tailor ChatGPT's responses to particular needs or preferences, enhancing its utility in various applications.
  - **Integration Capabilities:** ChatGPT integrates seamlessly with applications, websites, and messaging platforms, offering conversational capabilities across different digital channels.

2. DALL·E

- **Overview:**

  - **DALL·E** is an image generation model that creates visual content from textual descriptions. It is designed to generate high-resolution images that match the provided prompts, exploring creative possibilities.

- **Technological Aspects:**

  - **Architecture:** DALL·E uses a variant of the GPT model adapted for image generation. It combines natural language processing with generative adversarial networks (GANs) to translate text into images.

- **Training Data:** The model is trained on a large dataset of text-image pairs, allowing it to learn the relationship between textual descriptions and visual features. It uses techniques like contrastive learning to improve its image synthesis capabilities.

- **Real-World Use Cases:**

  - **Creative Design:** Artists and designers use DALL·E to generate unique visual concepts, illustrations, and artwork based on textual descriptions. It aids in exploring new design ideas and visual styles.
  - **Marketing and Advertising:** DALL·E creates customized visuals for marketing campaigns, advertisements, and social media posts. It helps in generating eye-catching graphics that align with specific themes and messages.
  - **Product Visualization:** Businesses use DALL·E to visualize product concepts and prototypes, providing realistic images based on design specifications and descriptions.

- **Features and Innovations:**

  - **Text-to-Image Synthesis:** DALL·E generates images from textual prompts, offering a novel approach to visual content creation. It can produce diverse and imaginative images based on user input.
  - **High-Resolution Output:** The model produces detailed and high-quality images, ensuring that the

generated visuals meet professional standards.

- **Creative Exploration:** DALL·E allows users to experiment with different artistic styles and concepts, facilitating creative exploration and innovation.

3. Codex

- **Overview:**

  - **Codex** is a code generation model developed by OpenAI, specifically designed to assist with programming tasks. It powers tools like GitHub Copilot, providing intelligent code suggestions and completions.

- **Technological Aspects:**

  - **Architecture:** Codex is built on the GPT-3 architecture, with modifications for code generation. It is trained on a diverse dataset of code and natural language, enabling it to understand and generate code across various programming languages.
  - **Training Data:** Codex is trained on a large corpus of publicly available code from sources like GitHub, allowing it to learn coding patterns, syntax, and best practices.

- **Real-World Use Cases:**

  - **Code Completion:** Codex assists developers by suggesting code snippets and completing code segments in real-time. It helps in writing code more efficiently and reduces the time spent on repetitive tasks.

- ○ **Documentation Generation:** The model generates documentation and comments for codebases, improving code readability and maintainability. It can automatically generate docstrings and explanations based on code structure.
- ○ **Learning and Tutoring:** Codex supports learning and skill development by providing code examples, explanations, and assistance to new programmers. It helps in understanding programming concepts and solving coding challenges.

- **Features and Innovations:**

  - ○ **Real-Time Code Assistance:** Codex provides context-aware code suggestions and autocompletions, enhancing productivity and reducing errors in coding.
  - ○ **Multi-Language Support:** The model supports a wide range of programming languages, including Python, JavaScript, Java, and more, making it versatile for different coding tasks.
  - ○ **Integration:** Codex integrates with IDEs like Visual Studio Code and platforms like GitHub, providing in-context code assistance and seamless workflow integration.

4.2 Microsoft Copilot

Microsoft Copilot offers advanced AI-powered assistance across various platforms and applications, significantly enhancing productivity and user experience. This section explores the integration of Copilot with

Windows and Office applications, providing a detailed look at its features and impact.

1. AI-Powered Code Assistance

- **Overview:**

  - Copilot is integrated into development environments like Visual Studio Code and GitHub, providing intelligent code assistance. It offers real-time code suggestions, autocompletion, and other features designed to streamline the coding process.

- **Integration with Visual Studio Code and GitHub:**

  - **Visual Studio Code:** Copilot is embedded within Visual Studio Code, a popular code editor used by developers worldwide. It provides context-aware code suggestions and completions as developers write code. The integration enhances productivity by reducing the need to manually type out code and by suggesting relevant snippets based on the current coding context.
  - **GitHub:** As a part of GitHub, Copilot leverages vast code repositories to offer intelligent code completions and suggestions. This integration helps developers access a wealth of coding examples and best practices, facilitating quicker development and reducing errors.

- **Real-Time Code Suggestions and Autocompletion:**

  - **Code Suggestions:** Copilot analyzes the code being written and provides real-time suggestions for code snippets, functions, and variables. These suggestions are context-aware, taking into account the surrounding code and programming language used.

- ○ **Autocompletion:** The tool offers autocompletion for code segments, reducing the time spent on manual typing and minimizing syntax errors. It speeds up the coding process by automatically completing common coding patterns and structures.

- **Enhancing Developer Productivity:**

  - ○ **Reduced Repetitive Coding Tasks:** Copilot automates repetitive coding tasks by generating boilerplate code and common patterns. This reduces the need for developers to write repetitive code manually, allowing them to focus on more complex and creative aspects of development.
  - ○ **Learning from Vast Code Repositories:** The model learns from a diverse range of code repositories, providing suggestions based on established coding practices and patterns. This helps developers write more efficient and high-quality code.

- **Impact on Software Development:**

  - ○ **Collaborating with AI in Programming:** Copilot represents a new paradigm in software development, where AI acts as a collaborative partner in coding. Developers can leverage AI assistance to explore new coding approaches, troubleshoot issues, and enhance code quality.
  - ○ **Considerations for Code Security and Privacy:** While Copilot offers valuable assistance, it is

important to consider the security and privacy implications of using AI in coding. Developers should be mindful of handling sensitive code and ensuring that proprietary information is protected.

2. Microsoft Copilot in Windows

Microsoft Copilot extends its capabilities beyond coding to enhance the overall user experience in the Windows operating system. The integration of Copilot in Windows provides a range of features designed to improve productivity and user interaction.

- **Overview of Integration:**

  - **Windows Copilot:** Integrated into Windows 11 and future versions, Copilot assists users with various tasks and workflows, offering AI-powered suggestions and automation to streamline interactions with the operating system.

- **Features and Innovations:**

  - **Contextual Assistance:** Copilot provides contextual assistance based on user activities and tasks. It offers suggestions for managing files, organizing documents, and optimizing system settings, making it easier for users to navigate and utilize Windows features.
  - **Task Automation:** The tool automates repetitive tasks such as file organization, system updates, and application management. Users can benefit from enhanced productivity by offloading routine tasks to Copilot.

- **Personalized Recommendations:** Copilot offers personalized recommendations based on user preferences and usage patterns. It helps users discover new features, applications, and tools that align with their needs and interests.

- **Real-World Use Cases:**

  - **File Management:** Copilot assists users in managing and organizing files, offering suggestions for file categorization, folder structure, and document naming conventions.
  - **System Optimization:** Provides recommendations for optimizing system performance, including adjusting settings, managing resources, and updating software.
  - **Application Integration:** Integrates with various applications to provide context-specific assistance, such as suggesting features or workflows based on the current task.

3. Microsoft Copilot in Office Applications

Microsoft Copilot enhances productivity within Office applications, offering AI-powered features to streamline document creation, data analysis, and collaboration.

- **Overview of Integration:**

  - **Office Copilot:** Integrated into Office 365 applications, Copilot assists users with tasks across Word, Excel, PowerPoint, and other Office tools. It provides contextual assistance, content generation, and data analysis capabilities.

- **Features and Innovations:**

  - **Word:**

    - **Content Generation:** Copilot assists in generating text for documents, including drafting content, suggesting improvements, and providing language enhancements. It helps users create professional-quality documents with minimal effort.
    - **Writing Assistance:** Offers grammar and style suggestions, ensuring that documents are well-written and polished. It also provides contextual recommendations based on the document's purpose and audience.

  - **Excel:**

    - **Data Analysis:** Copilot assists in analyzing data by suggesting formulas, generating charts, and providing insights based on data trends. It helps users make informed decisions and visualize data effectively.
    - **Automated Tasks:** Automates repetitive tasks such as data entry, formatting, and report generation, improving efficiency and accuracy in spreadsheet management.

  - **PowerPoint:**

    - **Presentation Design:** Offers suggestions for slide design, content layout, and visual enhancements. It helps users create visually appealing and effective presentations with minimal effort.

- **Content Generation:** Assists in generating presentation content, including text, images, and graphics, based on user input and presentation objectives.

- **Real-World Use Cases:**

  - **Document Creation:** Copilot supports users in creating a variety of documents, including reports, proposals, and essays, by providing content generation and editing assistance.
  - **Data Management:** Enhances productivity in data management tasks, such as data analysis, reporting, and visualization, by automating routine tasks and providing valuable insights.
  - **Presentation Preparation:** Streamlines the process of preparing presentations, offering design recommendations, content suggestions, and visual enhancements to create impactful slides.

4.3 Google's Gemini

Google's Gemini represents a significant advancement in natural language processing, offering powerful language capabilities and accessibility features.

- **Overview:**

  - **Gemini** is designed to enhance language understanding and generation, providing robust NLP capabilities for various applications.

- **Technological Aspects:**

- **Architecture:** Gemini utilizes advanced NLP techniques and models developed by Google, including transformer-based architectures similar to those used in GPT models.
- **Training Data:** Trained on a diverse range of text sources, Bard learns to generate and understand text with high accuracy and contextual relevance.

- **Real-World Use Cases:**

  - **Content Creation:** Gemini supports content creation by generating written material, including articles, reports, and creative writing, with a focus on coherence and quality.
  - **Translation Services:** Provides high-quality translations between languages, facilitating communication and localization efforts across different regions.
  - **Customer Interaction:** Enhances customer interactions by generating contextually relevant responses, supporting multilingual communication, and improving user experience.

- **Features and Innovations:**

  - **Contextual Understanding:** Excels in understanding and generating text with contextual awareness, making it suitable for a wide range of NLP tasks.
  - **Multilingual Capabilities:** Supports multiple languages, improving accessibility and communication for a global audience.
  - **Integration and Accessibility:** Gemini can be integrated into various applications and platforms,

providing language capabilities across different digital environments.

4.4 MidJourney and Stable Diffusion

MidJourney and Stable Diffusion are notable tools in the realm of artistic image generation, offering innovative approaches to creating visual content.

1. MidJourney

- **Overview:**

  - **MidJourney** is an AI-powered tool that generates artistic images from textual prompts, focusing on creating visually appealing and unique artwork.

- **Technological Aspects:**

  - **Architecture:** MidJourney employs advanced generative models and neural networks to translate text descriptions into images, incorporating artistic styles and creative elements.
  - **Training Data:** Trained on a diverse dataset of art and visual content, MidJourney learns to generate images that reflect various artistic styles and visual concepts.

- **Real-World Use Cases:**

  - **Creative Projects:** Artists and designers use MidJourney to generate original artwork and visual content for personal or commercial projects. It helps in exploring new artistic directions and styles.

- **Marketing and Branding:** Generates customized visuals for marketing campaigns, advertisements, and social media posts, enhancing visual appeal and engagement.
- **Concept Visualization:** Assists in visualizing creative concepts and ideas, providing a tool for brainstorming and design exploration.

- **Features and Innovations:**

  - **Text-to-Image Translation:** Converts textual descriptions into high-quality artistic images, offering a novel approach to visual content creation.
  - **Artistic Style Adaptation:** Adapts various artistic styles to the generated images, allowing users to experiment with different visual aesthetics and techniques.
  - **Creative Exploration:** Facilitates creative exploration by generating diverse and imaginative images based on user input.

2. Stable Diffusion

- **Overview:**

  - **Stable Diffusion** is a tool focused on generating consistent and high-quality artistic images from textual input, with an emphasis on stable image outputs.

- **Technological Aspects:**

- ○ **Architecture:** Utilizes generative models and diffusion techniques to produce images from text prompts, ensuring stability and consistency in image generation.
- ○ **Training Data:** Trained on a wide range of artistic content, Stable Diffusion learns to generate images that maintain visual coherence and quality.

- **Real-World Use Cases:**

  - ○ **Artistic Creation:** Enables artists to create unique visual content and explore new artistic styles, contributing to creative projects and design initiatives.
  - ○ **Media and Entertainment:** Assists in generating visual content for media, entertainment, and digital platforms, enhancing creativity and efficiency in content creation.
  - ○ **Personal Projects:** Used by individuals for personal artistic endeavors, including creating custom artwork and visual designs.

- **Features and Innovations:**

  - ○ **Consistent Image Generation:** Ensures stable and consistent outputs based on textual prompts, maintaining visual quality and coherence.
  - ○ **Customization Options:** Provides options for customizing image styles and details, allowing users to tailor generated content to specific needs.
  - ○ **Creative Flexibility:** Offers creative flexibility by enabling users to experiment with different artistic styles and visual concepts.

4.5 DeepMind's AlphaFold

DeepMind's AlphaFold represents a groundbreaking advancement in the field of structural biology, providing valuable insights into protein folding and function.

- **Overview:**

  - **AlphaFold** is an AI model developed to predict the 3D structures of proteins from their amino acid sequences, revolutionizing our understanding of protein folding.

- **Technological Aspects:**

  - **Architecture:** AlphaFold employs deep learning techniques and neural networks to predict protein structures with high accuracy. It uses complex algorithms to model the folding process and predict spatial arrangements.
  - **Training Data:** Trained on a vast dataset of protein structures and sequences, AlphaFold learns to predict protein folding patterns and interactions.

- **Real-World Use Cases:**

  - **Drug Discovery:** Facilitates drug discovery by providing insights into protein structures, aiding in the design of targeted therapies and treatments for various diseases.
  - **Disease Research:** Enhances research into diseases by elucidating protein structures associated with health conditions, supporting the development of new treatments and interventions.

- ○ **Structural Biology:** Advances the field of structural biology by providing accurate predictions of protein structures, contributing to a deeper understanding of biological processes.

- **Features and Innovations:**

  - ○ **High Accuracy:** AlphaFold achieves high accuracy in predicting protein structures, setting new standards in the field of structural biology.
  - ○ **Impact on Research:** Significantly impacts scientific research and drug development by providing valuable insights into protein folding and function.
  - ○ **Open Access:** AlphaFold's predictions are made publicly available, contributing to the broader scientific community and facilitating further research.

4.6 Runway ML

Runway ML offers a comprehensive suite of AI tools for creative professionals, focusing on video and image processing.

- **Overview:**

  - ○ **Runway ML** provides a range of AI-powered tools designed for video editing, image processing, and multimedia content creation.

- **Technological Aspects:**

  - ○ **Video and Image Processing:** Runway ML utilizes advanced generative models and neural networks for tasks such as object removal, background replacement, and style transfer.

- **Integration with Creative Software:** Integrates with popular creative software and platforms, enhancing workflow and providing seamless AI-powered capabilities.

- **Real-World Use Cases:**

  - **Creative Projects:** Used by filmmakers, designers, and multimedia artists to create and refine visual content for various projects, including films, advertisements, and digital media.
  - **Content Creation:** Assists in generating and editing content for social media, marketing campaigns, and entertainment, improving visual quality and engagement.
  - **Video Editing:** Provides tools for enhancing video content, including features for object tracking, scene transitions, and visual effects.

- **Features and Innovations:**

  - **Video Editing Tools:** Offers a range of tools for editing and enhancing video content, including object removal, background replacement, and style transfer.
  - **Image Processing Capabilities:** Provides advanced image processing features, such as color adjustment, object detection, and visual effects.
  - **Creative Flexibility:** Enhances creative flexibility by offering a diverse set of tools for multimedia content creation and manipulation.

4.7 Other Emerging Platforms

The generative AI landscape is continually evolving, with new platforms and tools emerging to address various needs and applications.

1. Jasper AI

- **Overview:**

  - **Jasper AI** (formerly Jarvis) is an AI-powered content creation tool designed to generate marketing copy, blog posts, and other written content.

- **Technological Aspects:**

  - **Natural Language Generation:** Utilizes advanced natural language generation techniques to produce high-quality written material based on user inputs and requirements.
  - **Content Templates:** Provides a variety of content templates for different purposes, including marketing, blogging, and social media.

- **Real-World Use Cases:**

  - **Marketing and Advertising:** Generates compelling marketing copy and advertising content, enhancing brand messaging and outreach.
  - **Content Creation:** Supports bloggers, writers, and content creators in producing high-quality written material efficiently and effectively.

- **Features and Innovations:**

- **Content Templates and Assistance:** Offers a range of templates and tools for generating written content, improving efficiency and quality.
- **SEO Optimization:** Assists in optimizing content for search engines, increasing visibility and engagement.

2. Writesonic

- **Overview:**

  - **Writesonic** is an AI-powered writing tool that provides content generation capabilities for various types of written material.

- **Technological Aspects:**

  - **Natural Language Processing:** Utilizes advanced NLP techniques to generate high-quality content based on user inputs and preferences.
  - **Content Templates:** Offers a variety of templates for different types of content, including blog posts, ads, and social media updates.

- **Real-World Use Cases:**

  - **Content Marketing:** Assists in creating engaging marketing content and advertisements, driving audience engagement and conversion.
  - **Creative Writing:** Supports authors and writers in generating ideas, developing content, and refining their writing.

- **Features and Innovations:**

- ◦ **Content Generation Templates:** Provides templates and tools for generating various types of content, enhancing efficiency and creativity.
- ◦ **Writing Assistance and Improvement:** Offers suggestions and improvements for enhancing the quality and effectiveness of written material.

Summary of this Chapter:

This chapter provides an extensive examination of key generative AI platforms and tools, including OpenAI's ChatGPT, DALL·E, and Codex, Microsoft Copilot, Google's Gemini, MidJourney, Stable Diffusion, DeepMind's AlphaFold, Runway ML, and emerging platforms like Jasper AI and Writesonic. Each platform is explored in detail, covering its technological aspects, real-world use cases, features, and innovations. The chapter highlights the transformative impact of generative AI across various domains, from natural language processing and image generation to code assistance and scientific research. By understanding these platforms, readers gain insights into the capabilities and applications of generative AI, as well as its broader implications for different industries.

CHAPTER V

The Importance of Data in Generative AI

Data is the foundation of generative AI, influencing how models learn and perform. This chapter provides an in-depth exploration of how data impacts generative AI, focusing on the role of large-scale datasets, challenges with data quality, and techniques for data augmentation and preprocessing.

5.1 Training Data: The Backbone of AI Models

1. The Role of Large-Scale Datasets

- **Foundation of Training:**

  - **Learning Mechanism:** Generative AI models learn patterns, structures, and relationships from large datasets. For instance, language models like GPT-4 are trained on diverse text corpora, enabling them to generate human-like text by understanding context, grammar, and semantics.

  - **Model Accuracy:** The accuracy and relevance of AI-generated outputs are directly proportional to the size and diversity of the training data. Large datasets provide a rich variety of examples, helping the model capture nuances and produce high-quality results.

- **Diversity and Representation:**

- ○ **Inclusivity:** To ensure the model performs well across various applications, the training data must represent different languages, cultures, and contexts. This inclusivity helps prevent the model from developing biases and ensures it can generate content relevant to a wide audience.
- ○ **Generalization:** A diverse dataset helps the model generalize from specific examples to broader concepts. This generalization is crucial for applications such as text generation, where the model needs to understand and produce coherent content across various topics.

- **Scalability:**

- ○ **Model Improvement:** As datasets grow, models often improve in their ability to generate accurate and contextually appropriate outputs. Larger datasets offer more examples for the model to learn from, enhancing its performance over time.
- ○ **Computational Requirements:** Training on large datasets requires significant computational resources, including powerful GPUs and extensive memory. The scalability of training infrastructure is a key consideration in managing large-scale AI projects.

- **Data Sources:**

- ○ **Web Scraping:** Automated tools and scripts gather data from websites, forums, and social media platforms. While web scraping provides a vast amount of data, it must be done ethically and legally, respecting copyright and privacy laws.

- **Public Databases:** Publicly available datasets, such as those provided by research institutions and open-source communities, serve as valuable resources for training AI models. Examples include Common Crawl and ImageNet.
- **Proprietary Data:** Organizations often collect proprietary data through user interactions, surveys, and internal processes. This data can offer insights specific to the organization's needs but must be handled with care to maintain privacy and security.

2. Ethical Considerations in Data Usage

- **Consent and Privacy:**

  - **Informed Consent:** Users whose data is used for training should be informed about how their data will be used and should provide explicit consent. This is essential for respecting individual privacy and complying with data protection regulations.
  - **Privacy-preserving Techniques:** Techniques such as anonymization and pseudonymization can help protect personal information while still allowing the data to be useful for training models.

- **Data Ownership:**

  - **Legal Rights:** Data ownership involves legal rights related to the use, distribution, and commercialization of data. Organizations must ensure they have the right to use data for training AI models and address any intellectual property concerns.

- **Attribution and Credits:** Proper attribution should be given to sources of data, especially when using datasets that are publicly available or sourced from third parties.

- **Transparency:**

  - **Data Provenance:** Providing information about the origins and nature of the training data helps users understand the basis of AI model outputs and fosters trust. Transparency includes disclosing data sources, collection methods, and any preprocessing applied.
  - **Ethical Guidelines:** Adhering to ethical guidelines and standards for data usage ensures responsible AI practices and helps mitigate risks associated with data misuse.

5.2 Challenges with Data Quality
1. Bias

- **Types of Bias:**

  - **Historical Bias:** Bias that stems from historical inequalities or prejudices present in the data. For example, if a dataset used for training a hiring algorithm reflects past gender imbalances, the model may perpetuate those biases.
  - **Sampling Bias:** Occurs when the dataset is not representative of the population it is intended to model. For instance, a medical dataset predominantly featuring one ethnic group may not generalize well to others.

- **Measurement Bias:** Arises from errors or inconsistencies in data collection methods. For example, if survey instruments are flawed, the resulting data may not accurately reflect the intended metrics.

- **Impact on AI Models:**

  - **Unfair Outcomes:** Bias in training data can lead to unfair or discriminatory outputs. For instance, a facial recognition system trained on biased data might have higher error rates for certain demographic groups.
  - **Model Performance:** Bias can also affect model performance, causing it to underperform in scenarios or for groups not well-represented in the training data.

- **Mitigation Strategies:**

  - **Data Diversification:** Actively seek and include diverse data sources to minimize bias and ensure balanced representation across different groups and contexts.
  - **Fairness Audits:** Conduct regular audits to identify and address biases in the model. This includes evaluating model performance across different demographic groups and implementing corrective measures as needed.
  - **Bias-aware Algorithms:** Utilize algorithms designed to mitigate bias, such as fairness-aware machine learning techniques that adjust for imbalances in training data.

2. Privacy

- **Data Sensitivity:**

  - **Sensitive Information:** Handling sensitive data, such as health records or personal identifiers, requires strict privacy measures to prevent unauthorized access and misuse.
  - **Anonymization:** Techniques such as data anonymization and pseudonymization help protect individual privacy by removing or obfuscating personal information.

- **Regulatory Compliance:**

  - **Data Protection Laws:** Adhere to data protection regulations such as GDPR (General Data Protection Regulation) and CCPA (California Consumer Privacy Act) to ensure compliance and protect user rights.
  - **User Rights:** Implement mechanisms for users to access, correct, and delete their data, in line with legal requirements and ethical standards.

3. Data Curation

- **Quality Assurance:**

  - **Data Cleaning:** Involves removing or correcting erroneous, incomplete, or irrelevant data. This ensures that the training dataset is accurate and reliable.
  - **Validation and Verification:** Techniques such as cross-validation and verification against trusted

sources help ensure the integrity and quality of the data used for training.

- **Data Relevance:**

  - **Contextual Appropriateness:** Ensure that the data is relevant to the specific application or problem domain. For instance, training a medical AI model requires data that accurately reflects medical conditions and treatments.
  - **Timeliness:** Keep the dataset up-to-date to reflect current trends, knowledge, and user needs. Outdated data can affect the relevance and accuracy of the model's outputs.

5.3 Data Augmentation and Preprocessing
1. Strategies for Improving Model Training

- **Data Augmentation:**

  - **Techniques:**

    - **Image Data:** Common techniques include rotations, translations, scaling, and adding noise. These augmentations create variations in the training data, helping the model generalize better.
    - **Text Data:** Techniques such as paraphrasing, synonym replacement, and contextual augmentation can increase the variability of text data, improving model robustness.
    - **Synthetic Data Generation:** Create new data samples using generative models or simulations. This can supplement real data and help balance

datasets.

- ○ **Benefits:**

  - **Increased Variability:** Augmentation introduces diversity in the training data, allowing the model to learn from a wider range of examples and scenarios.
  - **Enhanced Generalization:** By exposing the model to different variations of data, augmentation helps it generalize better to unseen examples and improve its performance on real-world tasks.

- **Preprocessing:**

  - ○ **Text Data:**

    - **Tokenization:** Splitting text into tokens (words or subwords) to facilitate processing and analysis.
    - **Normalization:** Converting text to a consistent format, such as lowercasing, removing punctuation, and handling special characters.
    - **Stop Words Removal:** Eliminating common words (e.g., "the," "and") that do not contribute significant meaning to the text.

  - ○ **Image Data:**

    - **Resizing:** Standardizing image dimensions to ensure compatibility with model input requirements.

- **Normalization:** Scaling pixel values to a consistent range (e.g., 0-1) to improve model training stability.
- **Augmentation:** Applying transformations to create diverse training samples and enhance model generalization.

- **Feature Engineering:**

  - **Extraction and Selection:**

    - **Feature Extraction:** Identifying and extracting relevant features from raw data, such as key phrases from text or keypoints from images.
    - **Dimensionality Reduction:** Techniques like Principal Component Analysis (PCA) to reduce the number of features while preserving essential information.
    - **Feature Scaling:** Normalizing or standardizing features to ensure that they contribute equally to the model's learning process.

2. Handling Imbalanced Data

- **Resampling Techniques:**

  - **Oversampling:** Increasing the number of examples in the minority class by duplicating existing samples or generating new samples using techniques like SMOTE (Synthetic Minority Over-sampling Technique).
  - **Undersampling:** Reducing the number of examples in the majority class to balance the dataset. This

involves randomly selecting a subset of majority class samples.

- **Synthetic Data Generation:**

  ○ **SMOTE:** An algorithm that generates synthetic samples by interpolating between existing minority class samples, creating new data points that help balance the dataset.
  ○ **Generative Approaches:** Using generative models to create synthetic data that mimics the characteristics of real data, enhancing dataset diversity and balance.

Summary of This Chapter

This chapter underscores the crucial role of data in generative AI, examining how large-scale datasets serve as the foundation for training effective models, the challenges related to data quality such as bias and privacy, and strategies for data augmentation and preprocessing. By addressing these aspects, organizations can enhance the performance, fairness, and reliability of their generative AI systems, ensuring they produce high-quality and ethically sound outputs.

CHAPTER VI

Introduction to Prompt Engineering

Prompt engineering is an essential skill for effectively utilizing generative AI models. It involves crafting inputs that guide these models to produce desired outputs. This chapter provides an in-depth look at the strategies for developing effective prompts, enhancing the quality of interactions with AI, and achieving precise results.

6.1 What is Prompt Engineering?

1. Crafting Instructions for Generative Models

- **Definition and Purpose:**

  - **Prompt Engineering:** The strategic crafting of inputs (prompts) that direct generative AI models to produce specific types of outputs. It is a critical practice for leveraging the full capabilities of AI in various applications.
  - **Importance:** Effective prompt engineering ensures that the AI understands the task at hand, leading to outputs that are more accurate, relevant, and creatively aligned with user intentions.

- **Designing Effective Prompts:**

  - **Clarity and Specificity:** Clear, detailed prompts reduce ambiguity, allowing AI to process requests more effectively. For instance, the prompt "Draft an email to a client explaining the delay in project delivery due to unforeseen technical challenges" directly guides the AI compared to a more ambiguous prompt like "Write an email about the project delay."

Examples of Effective Prompt Crafting:

- **Basic Inquiry:** "What is the boiling point of water?"

  - **Descriptive Prompt:** "Explain why the boiling point of water is 100 degrees Celsius at sea level."

- **Creative Content Generation:** "Generate a poem about winter."

  - **Detailed Creative Prompt:** "Compose a four-stanza poem in the style of Robert Frost about a snowy evening in the countryside."

2. The Impact of Prompt Quality on Output

- **Influence on Results:**

  - **Quality of Output:** The specificity and clarity of a prompt directly influence the AI's ability to produce precise and relevant responses. Well-crafted prompts result in outputs that closely match the user's needs.
  - **User Satisfaction:** High-quality prompts increase user satisfaction by reducing the need for repeated modifications and adjustments.

Illustrative Examples:

- **High-Quality Prompt:** "Provide a step-by-step comparison of photosynthesis and cellular respiration, highlighting their roles in the ecosystem."

  - **Output:** "Photosynthesis and cellular respiration are complementary processes in the ecosystem. Photosynthesis converts carbon dioxide and water into oxygen and glucose by using sunlight, primarily occurring in plants. In contrast, cellular respiration uses oxygen to convert glucose into carbon dioxide and water, releasing energy. This cycle supports life by providing energy and recycling crucial elements."

- **Poor Quality Prompt:** "Explain photosynthesis and respiration."

  - **Output:** "Photosynthesis and respiration are biological processes that plants and animals use to convert energy."

6.2 Basic Prompt Structures
1. Simple vs. Complex Prompts
Simple Prompts:

- **Definition:** Direct prompts that require straightforward answers or minimal depth. They are best for quick queries or when a concise response is needed.
- **Examples:**

  - **Simple Inquiry:** "Who wrote Macbeth?"

    - **Output:** "Macbeth was written by William Shakespeare."

Complex Prompts:

- **Definition:** Intricately designed prompts that require detailed responses or involve multiple elements. They are used when depth, explanation, or creative output is needed.
- **Examples:**

  - **Complex Instruction:** "Outline the causes of the French Revolution, incorporating economic, social, and political factors, and discuss its impact on European politics."

    - **Output:** "The French Revolution was driven by a combination of economic distress, social inequality, and political mismanagement. Economically, the common populace suffered under heavy taxation and food scarcity while the aristocracy lived lavishly. Socially, Enlightenment ideas challenged traditional hierarchies and monarchies. Politically, King Louis XVI's inability to solve fiscal crises led to widespread discontent. The revolution radically altered European politics by promoting republicanism over monarchism, influencing subsequent revolutions across the continent."

2. Layering Prompts for Detailed Responses

- **Layered Prompts:** These prompts combine multiple questions or directives into a single, structured prompt to extract detailed and multi-faceted responses.
- **Example:**

- ○ **Layered Prompt:** "Develop a comprehensive marketing strategy for a new health drink targeting millennials. Include market analysis, product positioning, promotional strategies, and anticipated challenges."

  - ▪ **Output:** "The marketing strategy for the new health drink should focus on millennials by highlighting wellness and convenience. Market analysis indicates a growing trend in health consciousness among this demographic. The product should be positioned as both nutritious and convenient, ideal for busy lifestyles. Promotional strategies should leverage social media and influencer partnerships to build brand awareness. Anticipated challenges include stiff competition from established brands and the need for distinctive branding to capture market share."

6.3 Context-Aware Prompts
1. Providing Sufficient Context for Models

- **Importance of Context:** Context enriches prompts by giving AI models background information or frameworks within which to generate responses. This enhances the relevance and accuracy of the output.
- **Example with Context:**

  - ○ **Context-Aware Prompt:** "Given the increase in remote work due to global health concerns, assess the long-term viability of remote work models in tech industries, considering productivity, employee satisfaction, and organizational culture."

- **Output:** "The long-term viability of remote work in tech industries appears promising. Productivity levels have remained stable or improved due to fewer in-office distractions. Employee satisfaction has benefited from flexible work arrangements, though challenges persist in maintaining an inclusive organizational culture. Companies may need to invest in virtual team-building and communication technologies to sustain these models."

2. Examples of Context-Aware Prompts

- **Detailed Prompt:** "Analyze the impact of the recent trade policy changes between the U.S. and China on global supply chains, particularly in the electronics sector, considering factors like manufacturing, pricing, and consumer access."

  - **Output:** "The recent trade policy changes between the U.S. and China have had significant impacts on global supply chains, especially in the electronics sector. Manufacturing has faced disruptions due to tariffs and trade barriers, leading to increased production costs. These costs have been passed on to consumers, affecting pricing and access. Companies are adapting by diversifying their manufacturing locations and reevaluating their supply chain strategies to mitigate risks."

6.4 Prompt Experimentation and Iteration

1. Testing and Refining Prompts

- **Iterative Process:** The practice of continuously testing and refining prompts based on the outputs received. This process helps in honing the prompts to achieve more precise and applicable results.
- **Example of Iteration:**

  - **Initial Prompt:** "Discuss the role of artificial intelligence in modern healthcare."

    - **Output:** "Artificial intelligence plays a significant role in modern healthcare by enhancing diagnostic accuracy, personalizing treatment plans, and improving patient management."

  - **Refined Prompt:** "Evaluate the specific applications of AI in diagnosing cardiovascular diseases, including the technologies used and the benefits over traditional diagnostic methods."

    - **Output:** "AI applications in diagnosing cardiovascular diseases include the use of machine learning algorithms to analyze cardiac images and detect anomalies. Technologies such as AI-enhanced echocardiograms and wearable monitors provide more accurate and timely diagnostics compared to traditional methods. These AI-driven approaches enable earlier detection of cardiovascular conditions, potentially leading to better patient outcomes and reduced healthcare costs."

2. Iterative Improvement Techniques

- **Feedback Loop:** Incorporating feedback from the outputs to refine the prompt structure, content, and specificity. This loop is crucial for aligning the AI's responses with user expectations and requirements.
- **Example of Feedback-Based Refinement:**

  - **First Prompt:** "Write a guide on using solar panels for home energy needs."

    - **Output:** "Solar panels can be installed on rooftops to convert sunlight into electricity, reducing reliance on traditional energy sources and decreasing utility bills."

  - **Refined Prompt:** "Create a detailed homeowner's guide on installing solar panels, including cost analysis, potential savings, installation procedures, and maintenance tips."

    - **Output:** "Installing solar panels involves several steps, including assessing your home's solar potential, choosing the right type of panels, and finding a reputable installer. Costs can vary based on panel quality and installation complexity but typically range from $10,000 to $25,000. Homeowners may see substantial savings on energy bills, often recovering costs within 7 to 15 years. Regular maintenance involves cleaning panels and monitoring for efficiency. This guide provides comprehensive information to help homeowners make informed decisions about solar energy investments."

Summary of This Chapter

This Chapter thoroughly explores the strategic crafting of prompts for generative AI models, emphasizing the importance of clarity, context, and continuous refinement. Through detailed examples and iterative techniques, this chapter equips readers with the knowledge to effectively guide AI models, enhancing the quality and relevance of generated outputs. By mastering prompt engineering, users can unlock the full potential of generative AI across various applications.

CHAPTER VII

Advanced Prompt Engineering with Examples

This chapter delves deeper into the art and science of prompt engineering, exploring sophisticated techniques and diverse examples that demonstrate how to effectively guide generative AI models. Each section includes practical, creative, and complex examples tailored to specific applications in text, image, and audio generation.

7.1 Prompts for Text Generation (e.g., ChatGPT)

1. Conversational Prompts

- **Purpose and Strategy:**

  - Designed to engage AI in a dialogue that mimics human interaction. Useful for creating dynamic and context-aware chatbots and virtual assistants.

- **Examples:**

  - **Customer Service Bot Prompt:** "A customer is asking about their order status that was delayed. Respond politely and offer a solution."

    - **Output:** "I'm sorry for the delay in your order. It's on the way and should arrive by tomorrow. We appreciate your patience and would like to offer you a 10% discount on your next purchase as an apology for the inconvenience."

- ○ **Health Advice Bot Prompt:** "A user asks for simple exercises for staying active during the workday. Provide friendly and practical suggestions."

  - ▪ **Output:** "Taking short breaks to stretch or walk around can make a big difference! Try setting a reminder to stand up every hour, or perhaps a few gentle stretches at your desk could be helpful. Keeping a small set of dumbbells nearby for quick arm exercises is also a great idea."

2. Creative Writing and Storytelling Prompts

- **Purpose and Strategy:**

  - ○ To inspire creativity and generate fiction, scripts, or poetry. These prompts need to be rich in detail to guide the AI towards the desired narrative tone and style.

- **Examples:**

  - ○ **Fantasy Story Prompt:** "Write a story about a knight who rescues a dragon from humans. Set the scene in a mythical forest and include elements of friendship and adventure."

    - ▪ **Output:** "In the twilight shadows of Eldwood Forest, Sir Cedric, the knight famed more for his compassion than his combat, stumbled upon a rare sight—a dragon ensnared by human hunters. Unlike his brethren who would slay a dragon without thought, Cedric chose to free the magnificent creature, forging an unlikely friendship that led to grand adventures across the mystical lands of Eldoria."

- ○ **Poetry Prompt:** "Compose a poem about the solitude of space travel, using a melancholic tone and rich imagery."

  - ▪ **Output:** "Amongst the starlit void I sail, alone,/A solitary voyager on a silent throne./Endless galaxies in solemn rows pass by,/Each star a distant tear the universe won't cry."

3. Code Generation Examples

- **Purpose and Strategy:**

  - ○ To assist in software development by generating functional programming code based on specifications or solving coding problems.

- **Examples:**

  - ○ **Web Development Prompt:** "Generate HTML and CSS for a responsive contact form with name, email, and message fields."

    - ▪ **Output:**

```
"<html>
  <head>
  <style>
```

```
form { max-width: 500px; margin: auto; }
input, textarea { width: 100%; margin: 10px 0; }
</style>
</head>
<body>
<form>
<input type="text" name="name"
placeholder="Your Name" required>
<input type="email" name="email"
placeholder="Your Email" required>
<textarea name="message" placeholder="Your
Message" required></textarea>
<button type="submit">Send</button>
</form>
</body>
</html>"
```

- **Algorithm Prompt:** "Create a Python function to reverse a linked list."

  - **Output:**

```
"class ListNode:
    def __init__(self, value=0, next=None):
    self.value = value
    self.next = next
    def reverse_linked_list(head):
    prev = None
    current = head
    while current:
    next = current.next
    current.next = prev
```

> *prev = current*
> *current = next*
> *return prev* **"**

7.2 Prompts for Image Generation (e.g., DALL·E, MidJourney)

1. Descriptive Prompts for Art and Design

- **Purpose and Strategy:**

  - To create specific visual content by providing detailed descriptions that include subject matter, artistic style, colors, and mood.

- **Examples:**

  - **Artistic Visualization Prompt:** "Generate an image of an ancient tree with sprawling roots, covered in glowing fungi, under a starry night sky, in a surrealistic style."

    - **Output:** The AI creates a visually striking image that blends the mystical elements of a surrealistic landscape with the natural beauty and mystique of an ancient, luminescent tree under a star-studded sky.

  - **Fashion Design Prompt:** "Design a futuristic evening gown that incorporates metallic fabrics and LED lights, suitable for a high-fashion runway."

    - **Output:** The AI generates a concept image of a sleek, shimmering gown with intricate patterns of

LED lights, combining modern technology with high fashion.

2. Stylization and Creative Control

- **Purpose and Strategy:**

  - To manipulate and guide the artistic process by specifying styles or creative interpretations in the prompt.

- **Examples:**

  - **Historical Stylization Prompt:** "Create a portrait of a modern-day woman as if painted by Johannes Vermeer, focusing on lighting and facial expressions reminiscent of 'Girl with a Pearl Earring'."

    - **Output:** The AI produces a portrait that echoes Vermeer's soft lighting and intimate portrayal, updated with modern attire and aesthetics.

  - **Abstract Art Prompt:** "Generate an abstract painting that represents the concept of chaos, using vibrant colors and dynamic, swirling patterns."

    - **Output:** The AI delivers an artwork filled with explosive colors and forms that visually depict the tumult and disorder of chaos.

7.3 Prompts for Audio and Music Generation
1. Structuring Prompts for Sound Creation

- **Purpose and Strategy:**

  - To produce specific types of sounds or music, incorporating elements like tone, rhythm, and instrumentation.

- **Examples:**

  - **Ambient Soundtrack Prompt:** "Create a 3-minute ambient soundtrack that incorporates the sounds of a rainforest at dawn, including bird calls, a gentle breeze, and a distant waterfall."

    - **Output:** The AI synthesizes a serene audio landscape that immerses the listener in the early morning ambiance of a lush rainforest.

  - **Cinematic Score Prompt:** "Compose a dramatic orchestral piece suitable for a movie climax scene, featuring a crescendo of strings and a powerful brass finale."

    - **Output:** The AI crafts an orchestral score that builds tension with a rising string section, culminating in a grand brass climax, perfect for a film's pivotal moment.

2. Genre-Specific Prompts

- **Purpose and Strategy:**

  - To guide the AI in creating music that fits specific genres, detailing stylistic elements, tempo, and mood.

- **Examples:**

  - **Jazz Music Prompt:** "Generate a smooth jazz track that features a saxophone solo, light piano accompaniment, and a relaxed tempo, suitable for a cozy evening."

    - **Output:** The AI composes a smooth jazz piece with a sultry saxophone melody, understated piano chords, and a laid-back rhythm, ideal for unwinding.

  - **Electronic Dance Music Prompt:** "Produce an upbeat electronic dance music (EDM) track with high energy synth beats, a catchy bassline, and drops for dance floor vibes."

    - **Output:** The AI develops an energetic EDM track that features pulsating synths, a driving bassline, and dynamic drops, creating the perfect soundtrack for a night out dancing.

7.4 Task-Specific Prompts

1. Prompts for Summarization, Translation, Data Extraction

- **Purpose and Strategy:**

  - Designed to perform specific tasks efficiently, these prompts must be clear and directed to achieve accurate results.

- **Examples:**

  - **Summarization Prompt:** "Summarize the key points from the 2021 UN Climate Change Conference, focusing on major agreements and future commitments."

    - **Output:** "The 2021 UN Climate Change Conference concluded with significant agreements among nations to accelerate emissions reductions, enhance transparency in reporting, and increase financial support for climate change mitigation in developing countries. Key commitments include phasing out coal, reducing deforestation, and aiming for more ambitious national emission reduction targets by 2030."

  - **Translation Prompt:** "Translate the following technical manual excerpt from English to German: 'Ensure the device is powered off before attempting any maintenance.'"

    - **Output:** "Stellen Sie sicher, dass das Gerät ausgeschaltet ist, bevor Sie Wartungsarbeiten versuchen."

  - **Data Extraction Prompt:** "Extract all statistical data regarding market share and revenue growth from the provided business report."

    - **Output:** "Market Share: 20% increase year-over-year; Revenue Growth: 15% increase in the last quarter."

Summary of this Chapter

The Chapter enhances your understanding of how to effectively employ advanced prompt engineering techniques across different media. This chapter provides a wealth of examples that illustrate the art of crafting detailed and strategic prompts to maximize the potential of generative AI in producing tailored, high-quality outputs. By mastering these techniques, users can extend the capabilities of AI to create innovative solutions and compelling content across various fields.

CHAPTER VIII

The Ethics of Generative AI

As generative AI continues to evolve and integrate into various sectors, ethical considerations become paramount. This chapter discusses the moral implications of generative AI technologies, focusing on issues such as bias and fairness, copyright and plagiarism, potential misuse, and the need for transparency and accountability.

8.1 Bias and Fairness in Generative AI Models

1. Identifying and Addressing Biases in Outputs

- **Challenges of Bias:**

  - **Sources of Bias:** Biases in generative AI models often stem from the data on which they are trained. If the training data contain historical prejudices or skewed perspectives, the model's outputs can perpetuate these biases.
  - **Impact on Society:** Unaddressed biases can lead to unfair treatment of certain groups, reinforcing stereotypes and contributing to inequality.

- **Strategies for Mitigation:**

  - **Diverse Data Sets:** Ensuring that training data are diverse and representative of different groups can help mitigate biases.
  - **Regular Audits:** Implementing routine audits of AI outputs to identify and address biases systematically.

- **Example:** An AI model used for hiring might show a preference for male candidates over female candidates due to historical data trends. By auditing this output and adjusting the training dataset or model parameters, developers can work towards a more equitable AI system.

2. Ethical Considerations in the Deployment of AI Systems

- **Deployment Ethics:**

  - **Considerate Implementation:** When deploying AI systems, it is crucial to consider the potential impacts on all stakeholders, including those indirectly affected.
  - **Ethical Guidelines:** Developing and following ethical guidelines to ensure that AI systems do not harm users or the public.

- **Example:** Before deploying an AI system in a healthcare setting, it's essential to assess its potential impacts on patient privacy, treatment accuracy, and accessibility of care.

8.2 Plagiarism and Copyright Issues
1. Legal Implications of Generated Content

- **Copyright Concerns:**

  - **Content Ownership:** Determining the ownership of AI-generated content can be complex, especially when such content closely resembles human-created originals.

- ◦ **Legal Challenges:** The legal landscape for AI-generated content is still evolving, with ongoing debates around copyright law applicability.

- **Example:** An AI that composes music might inadvertently create melodies that resemble copyrighted songs, leading to legal challenges from original creators.

2. Originality vs. Training Data

- **Training Data Influence:**

  - ◦ **Influence on Output:** The content produced by generative AI models is often reflective of the data used in training. This raises questions about the originality of the outputs.
  - ◦ **Originality Issues:** Distinguishing between truly original content and that which is heavily derived from training data is a challenge for creators and copyright holders alike.

- **Example:** If a generative AI model trained on popular novels writes a book, how much of that book is new creation, and how much is a recombination of its training data?

8.3 Misuse of AI-Generated Content

1. **Deepfakes, Misinformation, and Malicious Applications**

- **Risks of Misuse:**

- ◦ **Deepfakes:** AI-generated images, videos, or audio that mimic real people, potentially used to spread misinformation or harm reputations.
- ◦ **Misinformation:** AI tools that generate believable but false content can exacerbate issues of fake news and misinformation.

- **Example:** Deepfake technology could be used to create a video of a public figure making false statements, potentially influencing public opinion or causing personal harm.

2. Preventing Misuse

- **Regulations and Controls:**

  - ◦ **Monitoring and Regulations:** Implementing strict monitoring and regulatory frameworks to prevent the misuse of AI technologies.
  - ◦ **Awareness and Education:** Educating the public and AI users about the potential for misuse can help mitigate risks associated with AI-generated content.

8.4 Transparency and Accountability
1. Explainability in Generative AI Systems

- **Importance of Explainability:**

  - ◦ **Understanding AI Decisions:** For AI systems to be trusted, users and regulators must understand how decisions are made, especially in critical areas like healthcare or law enforcement.

- **Improving Trust:** Transparent AI processes help build trust among users and stakeholders, ensuring that AI solutions are adopted more widely.

- **Example:** An AI system used in loan approval should be able to explain its decisions to applicants, detailing why a particular loan was approved or denied based on understandable criteria.

2. Ensuring Accountability

- **Measures for Accountability:**

  - **Audit Trails:** Keeping detailed logs of AI decisions to trace outputs back to their origins in data or model behavior.
  - **Legal and Ethical Standards:** Establishing clear legal and ethical standards for AI development and use, ensuring developers and companies are held accountable for their systems.

- **Example:** In the case of an autonomous vehicle accident, audit trails can help determine whether the AI or human error was at fault, aiding in legal and repair processes.

Summary of this Chapter

This Chapter explores the complex ethical landscape surrounding generative AI technologies. By addressing bias, copyright issues, potential misuse, and the importance of transparency and accountability, this chapter aims to equip readers with the knowledge to navigate and address ethical challenges in AI effectively. Through careful consideration and ethical practice, the benefits of generative AI can be maximized while minimizing harm to individuals and society.

91

CHAPTER IX

The Future of Generative AI

This chapter explores the evolving landscape of generative AI, looking at recent advances and potential future developments that could redefine how we interact with technology across various sectors. It highlights the expansion of multimodal models, the role of AI in scientific discovery, the convergence with other cutting-edge technologies, and the broader implications for society.

9.1 Advances in Multimodal Models

1. Models that Combine Text, Image, and Video

- **Definition and Impact:**

  - **Multimodal Models:** AI systems that integrate and process multiple types of data (text, images, video, etc.) simultaneously. These models offer a more holistic approach to understanding and generating content that mirrors human sensory and cognitive abilities.

- **Examples and Applications:**

  - **Enhanced Interaction:** Multimodal models can interpret a scene in a video, transcribe spoken words, and generate relevant textual responses, providing a seamless interactive experience for users in educational and customer service applications.
  - **Creative Content Production:** These models assist in the creation of complex media, such as generating a

video from a script or converting a storyline into a fully animated short film.

- **Future Prospects:**

  - **Integration in Everyday Devices:** Future advancements may lead to more intuitive interactions with personal devices and smart home systems, where commands can be given in any form—spoken, written, or visual.

9.2 Generative AI in Scientific Discovery
1. Applications in Chemistry, Biology, and Physics

- **Innovative Contributions:**

  - **Drug Discovery:** Generative AI models accelerate the design of new molecules with desired properties, significantly reducing the time and cost associated with developing new medications.
  - **Genetic Research:** AI helps in decoding genetic sequences with applications in personalized medicine and understanding genetic diseases.
  - **Material Science:** AI models predict new materials with specific properties for use in industries like semiconductors and renewable energy.

- **Impact on Research:**

  - **Speed and Efficiency:** AI's ability to quickly process vast datasets and simulate experiments can lead to faster scientific breakthroughs.

- ○ **Collaboration Enhancement:** AI tools that predict outcomes of experiments or propose new research avenues can foster collaboration across scientific disciplines.

9.3 The Convergence of Generative AI with Other Technologies
1. AI and AR/VR, Robotics, and Blockchain

- **Synergistic Developments:**

  - ○ **AI and AR/VR:** Generative AI enhances augmented and virtual reality experiences by creating more immersive and interactive environments, potentially transforming education, training, and entertainment industries.
  - ○ **AI and Robotics:** AI powers autonomous decision-making in robots, improving their ability to interact with the physical world in complex ways, such as in surgery or manufacturing.
  - ○ **AI and Blockchain:** AI can manage and optimize blockchain operations, enhance smart contract functionality, or predict cryptocurrency market trends.

- **Future Integrations:**

  - ○ **Holistic Technology Solutions:** The integration of AI with these technologies promises revolutionary changes in how we interact with digital and physical environments, leading to more personalized and efficient systems.

9.4 Opportunities and Challenges Ahead
1. The Future of Work, Creativity, and Productivity

- **Opportunities:**

  - **Work:** AI can automate routine tasks, freeing humans to engage in more creative and strategic activities, potentially reshaping job roles and industries.
  - **Creativity:** Generative AI opens new avenues for creative expression in art, music, writing, and design, providing tools that enhance human creativity.
  - **Productivity:** AI's ability to analyze data and automate complex processes can significantly enhance productivity in sectors like finance, healthcare, and logistics.

- **Challenges:**

  - **Ethical and Social Implications:** The displacement of jobs due to automation, privacy concerns, and the potential for AI-generated misinformation are significant issues that need to be addressed.
  - **Technological Barriers:** While AI technology is advancing rapidly, there are still considerable challenges in ensuring it works reliably and ethically in diverse real-world applications.

- **Balancing Act:**

  - **Navigating Progress:** The future will likely involve a delicate balance between leveraging AI for its benefits while managing its risks and ensuring it serves the broader interests of society.

Summary of this Chapter

This Chapter forecasts exciting advancements and challenges on the horizon for generative AI technologies. It discusses the integration of AI with various data modalities and technologies, its expanding role in scientific discovery, and the broader social and economic impacts. As AI continues to evolve, it promises to significantly alter our world, presenting both unprecedented opportunities and challenges that will require careful consideration and management.

Conclusion: Embracing Generative Ai

As we conclude this exploration into the world of generative AI, it is evident that this technology is not just a tool of the future but a transformative force already reshaping our present. From creative endeavors to scientific research and everyday interactions, generative AI has begun to permeate various facets of human life. This final chapter summarizes the key concepts discussed throughout the book, reflects on how we can integrate AI more seamlessly into our daily routines, and considers the broader implications of AI as we look towards the future.

Summary of Key Concepts

Throughout this book, we've delved into the fundamentals of generative AI, understanding its mechanisms, applications, and the ethical considerations it entails. Key concepts include:

- **Prompt Engineering**: We learned the art and science of crafting effective prompts to guide AI models to produce desired outcomes, a skill crucial for leveraging AI's capabilities fully.
- **Ethical Considerations**: We explored the ethical landscape surrounding AI, including issues of bias, fairness, and the use of AI in creating deepfakes, emphasizing the need for responsible AI development and usage.
- **Multimodal Applications**: The discussion highlighted how AI is not limited to text but extends to generating images, audio, and complex interactive experiences, showing the versatility and expansive potential of AI technologies.

These concepts are foundational to understanding and navigating the evolving world of generative AI, providing a framework for both current applications and future innovations.

Adopting Generative AI in Daily Life

The integration of generative AI into daily life is already underway, and its presence will only grow stronger. Here are practical ways AI can become a more integral part of our everyday experiences:

- **Personal Productivity:** From AI-powered personal assistants that help manage schedules to sophisticated systems that automate routine tasks, AI can significantly boost personal productivity and efficiency.
- **Creative Expressions:** Whether it's composing music, writing stories, or creating art, AI tools provide individuals with new mediums and methods for creative expression, democratizing creativity and opening new avenues for amateurs and professionals alike.
- **Educational Tools:** Generative AI can personalize learning experiences, adapting educational content to fit individual learning styles and paces, making education more accessible and effective.

By embracing these tools, individuals and organizations can enhance their capabilities, streamline processes, and foster creativity, leading to greater fulfillment and efficiency.

Looking Forward: The Role of AI in Shaping the Future

The potential of generative AI to shape the future is immense and multifaceted:

- **Innovation Accelerator:** AI is poised to accelerate innovation across sectors by enabling rapid prototyping, automating complex processes, and deriving insights from large datasets.
- **Economic Transformation:** AI technologies are expected to transform economies, potentially leading to new industries and reshaping existing ones. While this transformation presents opportunities for growth, it also raises challenges, such as job displacement and the need for workforce retraining.
- **Societal Impact:** On a societal level, AI has the potential to address complex global challenges, such as climate change and healthcare. However, it also necessitates careful consideration of ethical issues, such as surveillance, privacy, and the digital divide.

As we look forward, it is crucial for policymakers, technologists, and the public to engage in continuous dialogue about the directions we want AI development to take and the values we want these technologies to uphold. Embracing AI is not merely about adopting new technologies but about steering these advancements in ways that promote the common good and mitigate potential harms.

Summary

Embracing generative AI involves understanding its capabilities, integrating its applications into daily life, and thoughtfully considering its broader implications. As this technology continues to evolve, it promises not only to enhance human abilities but also to challenge us to rethink our relationship with technology and its role in our future. This book aims to equip its readers with the knowledge to navigate this new era thoughtfully and responsibly.

Prompt Examples For Various Domains

In the world of generative AI, one of the most important factors that determines the quality and relevance of output is the design of the prompt. This chapter explores prompt examples across different professional domains, showcasing how AI can be applied to solve real-world problems and generate content, code, analysis, and strategies efficiently.

1. Content Creation

Generative AI has revolutionized content creation by allowing users to generate articles, reports, and summaries on any given topic. The effectiveness of the generated content often depends on how well the prompt is structured. A clear, concise prompt will lead to a more organized and meaningful output.

- **Prompt Example:**

  - **Task:** Develop a comprehensive 1000-word article on [specific topic].
  - **Prompt:** "Write a 1000-word article about the impact of remote work on productivity, including an executive summary, five key sections with subheadings, and a conclusion with actionable takeaways."
  - **Breakdown:** The prompt provides clear instructions on the word count, the structure (executive summary, key sections, and conclusion), and the topic (remote work and productivity). This gives the AI enough context to generate a well-structured and relevant article.

2. Software Development

In software development, AI can assist with generating code, explaining functionality, and creating documentation. By crafting precise prompts, developers can streamline coding tasks and improve efficiency.

- **Prompt Example:**

  - **Task:** Generate a Python class for [describe functionality].
  - **Prompt:** "Create a Python class for managing user authentication. Include methods for registering users, logging in, and logging out. Provide docstrings, inline comments, and example usage."
  - **Breakdown:** This prompt outlines the desired functionality (user authentication) and provides instructions for documentation and comments. The prompt's clarity ensures that the generated code is both functional and easy to understand.

3. Data Analysis and Visualization

AI can process large datasets and generate summaries, trends, and visualization strategies. By specifying what data needs to be analyzed and how to present it, you can get detailed, actionable insights.

- **Prompt Example:**

  - **Task:** Analyze the following dataset: [paste data].
  - **Prompt:** "Analyze the dataset on sales performance from Q1 2022. Provide a summary of key findings, identify significant trends, and suggest appropriate visualization techniques for presenting the results."

- ◦ **Breakdown:** This prompt includes a specific dataset, the analysis task (sales performance), and the output expectations (summary, trends, and visualization techniques). It ensures that the AI provides detailed and relevant analysis.

4. Marketing Strategy

Marketing involves creating and executing plans to engage customers and promote products. AI can help generate content calendars, social media strategies, and detailed marketing plans with proper prompt design.

- **Prompt Example:**

  - ◦ **Task:** Create a detailed social media content calendar for [brand/product].
  - ◦ **Prompt:** "Create a one-month social media content calendar for promoting a new fitness app. Include post ideas, optimal posting times, and relevant hashtags for platforms like Instagram and Twitter."
  - ◦ **Breakdown:** This prompt clearly defines the task (social media calendar), the subject (a fitness app), and the platforms (Instagram and Twitter), ensuring that the generated content is tailored to the appropriate audience and platform.

5. Business Communication

Business communication often involves writing professional emails, reports, or memos. By designing prompts that specify the tone, audience, and purpose of the communication, AI can assist in creating clear and concise business messages.

- **Prompt Example:**

  - **Task:** Compose a professional email to [stakeholder] regarding [specific business matter].
  - **Prompt:** "Write a formal email to the product development team regarding the delay in the new feature launch. Ensure clarity, conciseness, and an appropriate tone for the audience."
  - **Breakdown:** The prompt provides the subject of the email (delay in feature launch), the audience (product development team), and the desired tone, making it easier for the AI to craft an effective communication.

6. Strategic Planning

Strategic planning is essential for business growth and decision-making. With AI, you can generate SWOT analyses, competitive strategies, and long-term plans by crafting detailed prompts.

- **Prompt Example:**

  - **Task:** Develop a comprehensive SWOT analysis for [company/product].
  - **Prompt:** "Create a SWOT analysis for a tech startup launching a new productivity app. Provide detailed points for strengths, weaknesses, opportunities, and threats, and suggest potential strategies based on the analysis."
  - **Breakdown:** This prompt ensures the AI produces a structured and thoughtful SWOT analysis by clearly identifying the subject (a productivity app) and the sections required (strengths, weaknesses, etc.).

7. Financial Modeling

Financial modeling requires precise calculations and projections based on certain assumptions. Generative AI can assist in building models and financial plans by using well-structured prompts.

- **Prompt Example:**

  - **Task:** Outline the structure and key components of a 5-year financial projection model for [type of business].
  - **Prompt:** "Develop a 5-year financial projection model for a SaaS startup, including revenue forecasts, cost assumptions, and customer acquisition projections. Include essential metrics and assumptions."
  - **Breakdown:** The prompt specifies the type of business (SaaS startup) and the key components needed (revenue forecasts, costs, customer acquisition), providing clear instructions for financial modeling.

8. Human Resources

AI can be used to generate job descriptions, optimize hiring processes, and assist in HR-related tasks. Clear prompts can help draft detailed HR documents like job descriptions or performance reviews.

- **Prompt Example:**

  - **Task:** Draft a job description for [position].
  - **Prompt:** "Write a job description for a Senior Data Scientist. Include key responsibilities, required

qualifications, and a compelling company overview."
- ◦ **Breakdown:** The prompt outlines the job position and details the specific sections required (responsibilities, qualifications, company overview), ensuring the generated job description is complete and professional.

9. Legal Document Preparation

AI can assist in preparing legal documents by generating outlines, clauses, and summaries. With proper prompts, users can streamline the creation of agreements, contracts, and other legal materials.

- **Prompt Example:**

  - ◦ **Task:** Create an outline for a non-disclosure agreement (NDA) covering [specific area of business].
  - ◦ **Prompt:** "Draft an NDA outline for a software development company. List key clauses such as confidentiality, non-compete, and dispute resolution, and briefly explain their importance."
  - ◦ **Breakdown:** The prompt specifies the type of legal document (NDA) and the clauses needed (confidentiality, non-compete, etc.), helping the AI generate a structured and relevant outline.

10. Project Management

Project managers can leverage AI to design risk management plans, timelines, and project strategies. Prompts that clearly define project parameters and objectives ensure that the generated outputs are actionable.

- **Prompt Example:**

  - **Task:** Design a risk management plan for [project name].
  - **Prompt:** "Create a risk management plan for the implementation of a new CRM system. Identify potential risks, assess their impact and probability, and suggest mitigation strategies."
  - **Breakdown:** The prompt specifies the project (CRM system), the key sections (risk identification, impact assessment, mitigation), and provides clarity for AI to generate a useful risk management plan.

11. Customer Experience Enhancement

Improving customer experience involves mapping out customer journeys and identifying opportunities for improvement. AI can help streamline these processes with well-defined prompts.

- **Prompt Example:**

  - **Task:** Develop a customer journey map for [product/service].
  - **Prompt:** "Create a customer journey map for an online streaming service. Identify key touchpoints from sign-up to subscription, and suggest improvements to enhance customer satisfaction at each stage."
  - **Breakdown:** This prompt outlines the customer experience process, identifies key touchpoints, and asks for improvement suggestions, ensuring a comprehensive customer journey map.

12. Product Development

From generating product requirements to documenting technical specifications, AI can assist with various product development tasks. Structured prompts help guide AI to deliver clear and actionable content.

- **Prompt Example:**

  - **Task:** Generate a product requirements document (PRD) template for [type of product].
  - **Prompt:** "Create a PRD template for a mobile fitness app. Include sections for user stories, technical specifications, success metrics, and milestones."
  - **Breakdown:** The prompt provides clear instructions on the type of product (fitness app) and the components needed (user stories, technical specifications, etc.).

13. Operations Optimization

AI can help streamline operations by generating process flow diagrams and suggesting efficiency improvements. By crafting detailed prompts, users can receive actionable insights for operational improvements.

- **Prompt Example:**

  - **Task:** Create a process flow diagram for [specific business process].
  - **Prompt:** "Generate a process flow diagram for the order fulfillment process of an e-commerce business. Identify potential bottlenecks and suggest efficiency improvements."
  - **Breakdown:** The prompt specifies the business

process (order fulfillment), provides clarity on the desired output (flow diagram), and asks for optimization suggestions.

14. Market Research

Market research requires collecting data and insights to guide business decisions. AI can assist by generating questionnaires and analyzing survey data.

- **Prompt Example:**

  - **Task:** Design a comprehensive questionnaire for a market research survey on [product/industry].
  - **Prompt:** "Create a questionnaire for a market research survey on consumer preferences in the electric vehicle market. Include both quantitative and qualitative questions to gather insights on purchasing habits and expectations."
  - **Breakdown:** The prompt outlines the survey topic (electric vehicles) and asks for a mix of question types, providing clear guidance for AI to generate a useful questionnaire.

15. Sustainability Planning

AI can support businesses in creating sustainability strategies by helping generate actionable plans and measurable goals. Prompts that specify the goals and metrics make the generated strategies more practical.

- **Prompt Example:**

  - **Task:** Outline a sustainability strategy for [company/ industry].

- ○ **Prompt:** "Develop a sustainability strategy for a textile manufacturing company. Include short-term and long-term goals, key performance indicators (KPIs), and potential initiatives to reduce environmental impact."
- ○ **Breakdown:** This prompt clearly outlines the sustainability focus (textile manufacturing), the required elements (goals, KPIs), and the desired outcome, ensuring the generated strategy is actionable.

Glossary

Generative AI: AI models that create new content such as text, images, or music based on learned patterns from existing data.

Discriminative AI: Models that classify data into categories but do not generate new instances.

GPT (Generative Pretrained Transformer): A large language model designed to generate human-like text based on input prompts.

BERT (Bidirectional Encoder Representations from Transformers): A transformer-based model that understands the context of words in a sentence by looking at the entire sequence.

T5 (Text-to-Text Transfer Transformer): A model that treats all NLP (Natural Language Processing) tasks as text-to-text, including translation and summarization.

GANs (Generative Adversarial Networks): A generative model that uses two neural networks—one to generate data and another to distinguish between real and generated data.

VAEs (Variational Autoencoders): A type of generative model used to generate new data instances similar to the input data, often used in applications like image generation.

Diffusion Models: Generative models often used in image generation by reversing a noise process to generate new samples.

Multimodal Models: AI models capable of processing and generating content from multiple types of input, such as text and images, to produce richer, context-aware outputs.

Prompt Engineering: The process of crafting specific input prompts to guide generative AI in producing desired outputs.

Data Augmentation: A technique used to increase the amount of training data by creating modified versions of existing data (e.g., images or text) to improve AI performance.

Transfer Learning: A technique where a pre-trained model is adapted to a new task, reducing the amount of data required for training.

Zero-shot Learning: A method in which a model can recognize or generate data for classes it has not seen before based on learned similarities.

Fine-Tuning: The process of adapting a pre-trained model to a specific task by continuing training on a smaller dataset.

Transformer Model: A neural network architecture that uses self-attention mechanisms to process and generate sequences of data, revolutionizing NLP.

Self-Attention Mechanism: A technique in transformer models that helps focus on relevant parts of the input sequence to generate more contextually appropriate outputs.

Latent Space: The representation of compressed data that captures the essential features of the input, often used in VAEs and GANs.

Ethical AI: AI practices and implementations that consider fairness, transparency, accountability, and avoid harmful biases in models and data usage.

Explainability: The ability of AI systems to provide understandable and interpretable outputs that allow humans to understand the decision-making process.

Deepfakes: AI-generated synthetic media where a person in an image or video is replaced with another person's likeness, often used in malicious applications like misinformation.

Synthetic Data: Artificially created data that mimics real-world data, often used to supplement datasets for training AI models.

Bias in AI: The presence of systematic errors that result from imbalanced or flawed training data, leading to unfair or inaccurate predictions for certain groups.

Tokenization: The process of breaking down text into smaller pieces (tokens) to be processed by AI models, commonly used in NLP.

Reinforcement Learning: A type of machine learning where models learn to make decisions by receiving rewards or penalties based on their actions in an environment.

Supervised Learning: A type of machine learning where models are trained using labeled data to predict outcomes or classify data.

Unsupervised Learning: Machine learning that deals with finding patterns and relationships in data without predefined labels or outcomes.